*Animals in the Wild*

# Snake

*Mary Hoffman*

ISBN 0-590-41234-5

Text and illustrations in this form copyright © 1986 by Belitha Press.
Text copyright © 1986 by Mary Hoffman.
All rights reserved. This edition published by
Scholastic Inc., 730 Broadway, New York, NY 10003,
by arrangement with Raintree Publishers, Inc.

12 11 10 9 8 7 6 5 4 3 2      8 9/8 0 1 2 3/9

Printed in the U.S.A.
First Scholastic printing, May 1988

## SCHOLASTIC INC.

New York   Toronto   London   Auckland   Sydney

Most people don't like snakes and are afraid of
them. That is because many snakes are
frightening to look at, and some are poisonous.
But most of them, like this grass snake, are
harmless.

Most snakes lay eggs. Usually the mother snake leaves the eggs to hatch on their own. The baby snake is able to live by itself as soon as it breaks out of the egg. But unfortunately, many baby snakes are killed by animals.

This vine snake lives in Central America. When it senses danger, it raises its head and opens its mouth wide. In this way, it tries to scare away enemies.

This rattlesnake lives in the western United States. It has a very poisonous bite. When an enemy comes near, the snake rattles a warning noise with its tail.

A snake's poison is called venom. Venom is a liquid that flows down through the snake's fangs, its two upper front teeth. In the picture, someone is pressing behind the snake's head to make it release venom.

About fifty kinds of snakes live in the sea.
They are all poisonous, and their bite can be
dangerous. But they don't usually attack unless
they are frightened by swimmers. This snake
lives in waters near Australia.

Some snakes kill animals by squeezing them
tightly until they can no longer breathe. These
snakes are called constrictors. They include
boas, like the one in this picture, and pythons.

Some snakes, like the viper in this picture, have holes, called pits, on their faces. When the viper is near something warm, it feels the warmth with its pits. These pits help snakes find warm animals they can eat.

This mountain king snake from California eats
other snakes. When a snake's name has "king" in
it, that usually means it eats other snakes.

When one snake eats another, it can start from
the head or the tail. But when a snake eats
another animal, it swallows it headfirst so the
legs don't get caught in its throat.

Many poisonous snakes eat cold-blooded
animals like frogs and toads. After poisoning
a frog, this snake swallows it.

Constrictors often eat warm-blooded animals,
like this rat. The boa in this picture has its coils
around the rat as it begins to swallow it.

Snakes have special joints in their jaws that let them open their mouths very wide. This way, they are able to swallow their victims whole. But the python in this picture will not be able to swallow the crocodile — it is too large.

This nonpoisonous snake feeds only on birds' eggs. It swallows them whole. Because its jaws stretch open wide, it can swallow eggs that seem much too large. The snake does not digest the eggshell.

Once the snake has swallowed the egg, its
mouth closes. Muscles in the snake's throat
move the egg along and sharp bones crush the
eggshell. The snake spits out the shell and
swallows the rest of the egg.

Snakes move by contracting their muscles to
glide through the grass. Snakes in the desert
move in a different way, called sidewinding.
Using their head and tail for support, they lift
their body sideways.

Many snakes have protective coloring. Such camouflage helps them blend in with the background, keeping them hidden from enemies. This horned viper blends in with the desert sand of North Africa.

This tree snake from Thailand is camouflaged by its bright green skin. As you can see from the picture, snakes don't have eyelids. Clear scales cover their eyes, which are always open.

Snakes belong to a group of animals called reptiles. Most reptiles have scaly skin. When the scales become worn, the old skin is shed. This ladder snake from western Europe is shedding its skin.

Snakes spend most of their time alone. But they
do search for partners in order to mate. And,
sometimes, many different kinds of snakes sleep
together in a large group when the weather is
very hot or very cold.

A mongoose moves so quickly it can attack a snake
before it has a chance to strike. The mongoose in
the picture has killed a cobra. Many people also
kill snakes, even though snakes hardly ever attack
people. In fact, snakes are helpful because they
eat rodents that destroy crops.

In India, snake charmers use snakes to entertain
people. This cobra sways back and forth as the
man plays a flute. Because snakes have no ears,
the cobra cannot hear the music. It is swaying in
time to the man's movements. Snake charmers
treat their snakes well and often keep them as pets.

First published in hardcover in the United States of America 1986
by Raintree Publishers Inc., 310 West Wisconsin Avenue,
Milwaukee, Wisconsin 53203.

First published in the United Kingdom under the title
Animals in the Wild—Snake
by Belitha Press Ltd.,
31 Newington Green, London N16 9PU
in association with Methuen Children's Books Ltd.

Dedicated to Joss.

Scientific Adviser: Dr. Gwynne Vevers. Picture Researcher: Stella Martin.
Design: Ken Hatherley.

Acknowledgements are due to the following for the photographs used
in this book: Bruce Coleman Ltd pp. 4, 8, 9, 15, 16, 18, 19, 20, 21, and
22: Frank Lane Picture Agency Ltd pp. 2 and 14; Natural Science
Photos pp. 1, 3, and 10; NHPA pp. 5, 6, 13, 17, and 23; Oxford Scientific
Films pp. 7, 11, and 12. Front and back covers: Bruce Coleman Ltd.